Decoded

Dating   Relationships   Love

David L. Johnson Jr.

ISBN 978-0-615-38559-4

Published by Davis Boy Publishing

Dedicated to my daughter, Dajah.

Although a lot of the things that I talk about in my book are far too advanced for a six year old to read, I hope it will help, comfort and mentor you when the time is right.

Love,
Daddy

Decoded

Dating   Relationships   Love

{Table of Contents}

Introduction

Decoded is for anyone who would like to expand their knowledge of a mans thinking process and reasoning for their actions during dating & relationships.

I hope that women will put some of the information that I will be sharing in *Decoded* to use. This confidential information is often times heavily guarded by us men. We actually keep it hidden under lock & key, so take advantage of this granted permission into our minds & thoughts!

Ideally, using this book and applying it to your own life will help make dating a little bit easier, a little less confusing & a lot more fun! If you're in a relationship, you may be able to put some of my advice to use and keep the romance kindling.

Just think of *Decoded* as your own personal cheat sheet to men!

Decoded

{At the stop light}

Here's the first scenario. Each
woman on the planet has been put in this
predicament and it seems to piss them off
every single time it occurs...

You're riding along in your car with your
husband, boyfriend, fiance etc.

Everything is going perfectly. Seriously, the day could not go any better than what it is at this point. Then, you come to a stop at that dreadful red light. Stop lights always seem to cause conflict because of a lack of patience from your man. You're talking to your man about something important that has happened at work, school or even about the argument that you had with one of your friends. You're expressing yourself like no other. The matter is really concerning you and you feel the need to tell him all about it. While talking, you realize that you're not receiving any responses or feedback to your questions/statements that you are putting out there. So, you look over at him and he's in a daze. Everything on his body is as still as a statue except for his eyes that are moving slowly across the front windshield. You decide to turn and look at whatever it is that's completely taken over your mans mind, body & soul. Is it some kind of weird bug? When you turn to see what it is, it really pissed you off for a number of reasons. The first reason could be because you liked what you saw and therefore your man sure in the hell shouldn't. The other reason could be because it's flat out disrespectful. Anyhow, you look up and realize that it's not a foreign bug crawling across the windshield. Instead, it's another woman with a magnificent shape walking by in the crosswalk. She's wearing clothes that leave little for the imagination. But that doesn't matter because your man to the left of you seems to be using the hell out of his imagination anyway. As much as it may bother you, don't react. No snappy remarks, dirty looks or hitting! Simply don't let it bother you. For one, men are going to be men regardless of what you try to shape him into. You should rather have him look at a woman walking by while next to you, than to have him look at a woman, act on it and have relations while he is away from you. Besides, there is nothing better about a woman to a man than a confident, secure and jealous-free lady. Honestly, being cool, calm and collected will benefit you best in the long run. If you catch your man in a daze and that daze is controlled by a moving, wiggling ass or breast...be extra nice to him. Don't be nice to him because that is the right thing to do! Be extra nice to him because it will make him feel guilty for what he has done. Women seem to forget that men do have feelings and that they do have a memory bank. There is a proven way to help this problem. "Kill him with kindness." Just think about it...have you ever watched a man with his daughter or a very older brother with his very younger sister? Have you seen the way that the little girls love them with all of their heart? Good! Now, have you seen the way that the father or older brother responds to that? Think about it. The men treat those little girls like little princesses. All because those little girls love them unconditionally. No criticizing! No hitting! No attempting to control the father or brother...just simply love. Which leads me back to how women seem to forget that men have feelings and also memory banks. The reason why the father and older brother will bend over backward for that little girl is because he remembers all of the love she continued to give despite his flaws, under achievements or bad decision making. Even better, she never threw it in his face. That's what separates the respect you receive from the respect the daughter or little sister gets. That's something to think about. Right now, you're most likely saying, "I am good to him!!" Let me assure you, if you are thinking that-- then you are wrong and every time that piece of ass walks by... your man will continue to drool. Like I said before, men will be men but the question is, Can you stick to the program? Can you do all of the things that I will teach you to do throughout this book to change him into a loving man? A love man cares about how you feel and will put your feelings first. Regardless of his manly needs to watch sex appeal in motion, a loving man will at least try to fight the urge. Just keep reading and learn how to create a loving man without actually teaching!!

{Girls Night Out}

So you're out with your girlfriends on a Thursday night. You're normally the kind of girl that likes to stay at home and watch a movie. But on this particular night, you decided to go out anyway. You already know what the late night outing consist of when your girls go out. A

Decoded

bunch of horny people at the bar who can
barely speak or stand because of the large
of amount of alcohol they have taken in.
If not the bar, it's a night club where
another set of horny guys walk around
looking for a piece of ass. When you
walk by, you can somehow hear the
perverted things that the guys are saying.
Even though the music is blasting, the
words are loud and clear. Reading lips
are the worst thing a woman can do in
the night club. It's always some weird,
short, ugly guy who has the most to say.
Again, reading lips in a night club is the
most horrible thing a woman can do. It
seems to be the same lines being repeated
by the horny men in the club all night.
Things like, "Damn baby, you're lookin'

good tonight! Can I buy you a drink?" Or how about this line, "You have a phat ass! You gonna let me tap that?" Then, you get some really straight forward guys who come straight out and say, "Lets go back to my place and get it on."

Your girlfriends found themselves some guys to dance with and left you there in the corner completely alone. It's hot! Men and women smell like musk and you have to get up early the next morning. The night couldn't get any worse until this very handsome guy walks up to you and says, "I knew I shouldn't have come to this place. I have to get up really early tomorrow and my boys wouldn't stop bugging me to come along." Then he stands right next to you. He smells very good and he's not sweating. That indicates that he wasn't dancing with a bunch of different women. So, after standing next to each other for five whole minutes without any more words being said, you decide to break the silence. "Oh, you speak? I thought you were a mute," he replies. That simple but unique comeback makes you laugh. Before you know it, the club is closing. People are walking out of the exit doors. You begin to look around for your girlfriends but they are nowhere to be found. The charming guy is still standing right beside you then says, "Do you need a ride home?" You look around once more to see if you see your girlfriends. Still, they are nowhere to be found. You say to yourself, 'what the hell, I guess I'll get a ride home with him. He's nice, respectful and he smells good.' You also know that your girlfriends are with their little flings. On the car ride back to your place, the conversation continues to go perfectly. He's saying everything you want to hear. He's telling you how smart, pretty and different you are. You're soaking it up like a sponge. You arrive to your house and by this time, you feel like you've known him for years. With that being said, you invite him in. Bottles of wine are being popped open. One thing leads to another and the next thing you know, you're getting freaky with a total stranger. After sex, you both fall asleep in each others arms. The next morning you awake, he's already gone. On the pillow next to your head is a note that reads, "I had a wonderful time with you. Thank you for the fantastic night. P.S.- I took one of your business cards...call you soon. Yours truly, Joe Smith.

You take a deep breath and then place the note on your chest. Smiling from ear to ear, you turn to smell the sheets...hoping to smell a whiff of his cologne. A few days go by and you don't receive a call, so you continue on with your days of going to work and coming home late. You turn on your TV and make a microwave meal because you are too tired to make yourself a real dinner.

After taking a few bites of your TV dinner, you decide to put it in the refrigerator because it's slightly too cold. Annoyed by your exhaustiveness, which caused you to press the number one on the microwave instead of the number two, when heating up your meal. Then you close the refrigerator, leaving your microwave meal with the rest of the unfinished ones. Standing straight up, you then open the freezer and whip out the strawberry flavored Haagen Daaz ice cream. On the way to the couch, you kick off your heels, slide off your skirt and throw your matching blazer on the dining room chair. Eating your favorite ice cream, sitting on the couch wearing nothing but panties and a cream colored silk blouse... you begin to think, 'Why hasn't Joe called me yet. I really like him. We had a great connection. He likes me.' By the following week, your attitude about the situation begins to change. Now you're thinking, 'You know what.... fuck him, I don't need him. I was doing just fine before I met him and I will do just fine without him again.' By the third week, you begin to blame yourself just like all of the rest of the good women on the planet. 'Why isn't he calling? Did I do something wrong. We made love and he told me how much he cared about me.'

To get to that stage, you had to have done a lot of things wrong. That's okay because everyone makes mistakes. I'm

here to help you stop repeating it over
and over again. Here's the thing. Those
beautiful first few lines that he gave you,
were a part of his game. The whole, "I
knew I shouldn't have come to this place.
I have to get up really early tomorrow
morning and my boys wouldn't stop
bugging me to come along," line was said,
just to get you in bed. Don't get me
wrong, he thought you were cool but he
thought getting in between the sheets
with you would be even more cool. Also,
that five minutes of silence while he
stood right next to your sexy self..... that
was apart of his plan as well. Desperate is
never attractive, so he played it cool so
that you wouldn't place him in the same
category as you placed the other guys

that night in the club. The nice words on the ride home were said strictly to keep you blushing and to keep you feeling good. We all know that women love compliments and if you compliment them on something that you think they may not like about themselves... you're in. You're in their mind, body and soul. Only with time, the heart can be taken. So to answer you question that you sit around asking yourself....NO, NO, No & Yes, he does not love you. He does not want to marry you. He does not see a future with you and even if he did, you couldn't act on it because he most likely has a wife, girlfriend, kids to feed or commitment issues. Although, he did mean every word that he wrote in the letter. You can believe those written words because he wrote them from his heart. He knew that he would never call or talk to you again, so leaving you with some truthful words from the heart was easy and the least he could do.

Here's what you should do now. Continue going to work and doing the right thing. You open your heart and legs to a man who you thought really cared about you. There is nothing wrong with that. At least you didn't open your legs just because of lust. That's what hoes do. It's not your fault that you take love seriously and wear your heart on your sleeve. That's a gift. And it's not your fault that there are men out there that prey on women like yourself. So forget about him and know that everyone has a soul mate and you haven't met yours just yet. Or maybe you have and he's right in front of your face but God doesn't want you to realize it yet. Go to the gym and exercise. That can do things for you. It will keep you healthy, good looking and feeling confident. There is no better feeling than the feeling you receive after a hard workout.

{Is he Cheating on me?}

I often receive this question from women on a regular, "How do I know if my husband is cheating on me?" The answer to this question lies with you. It's proven that men often cheat when they're unsatisfied at home. Being a woman that is dedicated to satisfying her mans needs and raising children, is a superwoman

kind of job. Actually it's more than a
superwoman's kind of job when you
factor in cooking, cleaning & trying to
stay fit, etc...

There are some men who cheat because
of stupidity but most men cheat because
of the reason I stated above which is... for
being unsatisfied. I'm going to be
straight forward with you. If your man
has to ask you for a blow job....that's not a
good thing. First chance he gets, he will
cheat. No man should have to ask his
woman for such a thing. You should
already be willing and ready. I'm not
saying to go around and give blow jobs to
every guy that you date but the ones that
you see a future with.... you might want to
do that on a regular basis.

If you keep your home dirty and you don't take a shower everyday, he will cheat. He will go find a woman who smells good and keeps everything tidy. Just think about it... most men live like pigs. They come home, kick their shoes off and place their feet on the table. Then grab a beer, burp and dirty up everything he touches. He leaves all of the cabinets open after searching the entire kitchen for a glass to pour his beer in. Picture that! Now picture a woman doing the exact same thing. That sight would be horrible. Being a slob can't be done by both of you. A sloppy man always wants a neat woman because he knows and count on her to clean up after him just like his mother, grandmother and every other close woman in his life has always done. I'm not saying that you need to be a maid but I am saying to keep clean, personal hygiene wise and typical house cleaning wise. Don't scrub the kitchen floor with your toothbrush or anything but please do the laundry. Always make your man feel like the most strongest, coolest, nicest, passionate individual on the planet. A man is built on ego. He may often act like has has put his ego aside for different matters but don't let him fool you. His ego sticks with him like his own shadow. Everywhere he goes, you better believe that his ego is right there with him. Trust me when I tell you this, your mans ego is like his puppy from childhood and all you have to do is stroke it a few times to get him to love you forever. Also, wear sexy lingerie and during sex don't just sit there like a log. Men want to make love with a porn star. After all, sex is one of the number one things that crosses a mans mind on a regular basis. I know it may sound foreign to you but it's the truth. Take some time to watch and observe your man. Figure out what he likes and try your best to do all of those things without him knowing that you're trying. If he somehow figures out that you are doing all of those sexy, passionate and selfless things because you think that's what he likes...then he will not accept it at heart. He wants you to do those things because you chose to do them. He wants those

things to naturally come from within you.
The same way you want your man to
have a natural protector mode built inside
of him, is the same way he wants you to
have all of those things listed above.
You're probably thinking that's unfair,
but that's just how men are. You asked
and I answered. How about this... just try
those things for about two weeks without
the nagging or groaning and see how he
responds. I guarantee that your
relationship will begin to open up. Your
grumpy man will begin to smile,
understand and connect with you a lot
more. If you give all of yourself and he
still does not respond, dump him!
Divorce him! Forget about him! The
reason the consequence is so dramatic is

because if a man cannot recognize a woman who's doing right, he must only want a woman who's doing bad. So instead of lowering yourself to do bad things... just go. I know marriage is supposed to be forever but that promise was intended to be for God.

{Him and your Best Friend }

When you first met your man, you
were so happy to know that he was yours.
His smile made you feel so good and his
eyes had a sparkle in them that you just
can't explain. You both stay up talking
on the phone all night. Both of you
enjoyed every single second together.
Having him in your life made everything
okay. The love that you had in your heart

for him was unexplainable. You often tried to express the love, passion and understanding that you and your man shares to you best friends. I bet you already have a gut feeling as to where I'm going with this example, don't you? Your best friend has always been a really nice person to you and has always showed up whenever you called. But behind that big strong heart of hers she still carries a weak spot for men deep down inside. You know the best friend that I'm talking about. Most of the girls in high school disliked her because she was really good at eye contact. Using her eyes to seduce and hypnotize their boyfriends, actually excited her. Although she has never used her unique talent on any of the guys that you've liked or were involved with but her freaky ability still made you worry a bit. Anyhow, it's been years since high school and since then, she has changed her ways. What you failed to remember or understand is... just because people change their ways doesn't mean the energy of their old ways completely disappear. It still leaks through their pores, uncontrollably like the sweat on Kobe Bryants' forehead during the playoffs. It still has the potential to hypnotize.

While talking to your best friend about your new found love, she implies that she would like to meet him. You agree and set up a time for him to come over to your place. Thinking to yourself, 'What's the worst that could happen,' you call your best friend and give her the date and time to come over. You clean your house from top to bottom, especially your bedroom. If something was to happen between you and him on that night, you would want it to be in a clean house. You wore your favorite push up bra to show some cleavage but that didn't really matter to you because you were on your period. Cleavage is often used to start a sexual connection between people that will eventually lead to the next step. The next step for you was useless because of your period and that alone, began to irritate you.

Your best friend arrived early. She
seemed to look better than what she
normally looks like. She wasn't wearing a
new outfit or anything but her jeans
seemed to fit her perfectly. Her ass
looked so nice and round. Maybe she
over dried her jeans so that they would fit
more snug? Her breast looked so plump
and firm through her casual t-shirt, it
began to make you a tad bit jealous. It's
kind of crazy when you think back on it,
right? She wore the most "guyish" outfit
ever but it still made you think that your
man might like how it looked on her.
Then you begin to look her up and down
for no apparent reason.

Out of nowhere, the doorbell rings. Time

has quickly passed since your best friend arrived because you spent most of it pondering. As soon as he sat on the couch, you felt the connection between him and your best friend. After you introduced them to each other, it was like you vanished into thin air. They really enjoyed each others company. No flirting took place but what they were talking about was nothing like the things that you and him spoke of. Five minutes turned into ten minutes and they're still talking about a basketball game from last week. He and she seemed like a couple and that pissed you off. You walked into the kitchen, hoping they realized that you were gone. They didn't. They continued on talking an you could hear them loud and clear while slightly slamming the doors and dropping silverware into the sink. After a while, you walk back out into the living room.

You best friend notices the upset look on your face, then excuses herself from the great conversation that was taking place. Your man notices the whole insecurity thing that you are having and decides to tell your best friend to stay! That pisses you off even more because you feel that he cares too much about her feelings. Besides, who is he to tell your best friend to "stay?!" For one, it's your house and for two, they don't even know each other that well. With all of that running through your head, you finally break

down, "Can you guys just go?!" Unable to
explain yourself, you walk over to the
front door and open it. They both leave
with no question. After you closed the
door, you peeked out of the window to
make sure that they didn't stand outside
and talk to each other before leaving. To
your surprise, they went their separate
ways instantly after exiting. About a
week later, your man calls to see if you
are feeling completely fine. He tells
about how he ran into your best friend at
the movies. Even though she was
attending with a date, it still bothered you
that they were around each other without
you being present. So, you pick up the
guts to tell him to stop talking to your
best friend or you and him can't see each

other anymore.

He agreed and so did your best friend when you talked to her a while later. This whole situation has caused a slight problem between you and her because she doesn't think you trust her. Even though that might not be completely true, it's somewhere along those lines.

What you concluded was good because if you ask me what would've happen between your man and best friend if they would've have continued to talk....I would have definitely conclude sex between the both of them. Honestly, there is no reason why your man should be close with any of your girlfriends. When penis meets va-jay-jay (male meets female), a connection is automatically made. Even though they both may not realize it... it's there and could possibly turn into something that could hurt you and a lot of other people. Put it this way... all your man needs is a little stroking of the ego, something sexy to look at and a good smell to cheat. That's why it's your job to do those things before another woman comes along and does them.

{My Racist Dad}

Do you remember that one time when you were in love with a black guy? Actually, you may have not been in love, but you sure did like him a lot. Even though you both were complete opposites (appearance wise), you both understood each other from the inside out. Your dad taught you that at an early age. You know...that saying... "Never judge a book by it's cover." Your dad actually drilled that into you. But after you took his life long advice and only judged a book after reading it, he damn near disowned you. You and your black boyfriend did so many fun things together. He took you to his house and introduced you to his whole family. His old grandmother was one of the funniest people you'd ever met. She told you about how your boyfriend used to pee in the bed as a child. His grandma made you feel at home and like you were apart of the family. His mother was beautiful and looked young enough to be his sister. His dad was a hard working man who had great morals. It was clear where your boyfriend learned his values from.

The day he asked to meet your parents, you were so excited. You knew that your mom would take to him because she used to be a hippie in the late 60's, early 70's. Your mom dated a few black guys in her day and loved every second of it. Before getting pregnant with you and marrying your father, she was very verbal about those kinds of things. Although, your mom would click with him instantly, you really wanted your dad to meet him. Before your boyfriend arrived, your father was very happy and excited to meet him. He was curious to meet this guy that you have been doting about! Both of your parents were sitting on the couch when he knocked. Your little brother was sitting on the stairs, leaning forward so that he could see the front door. You opened the door and there he was! Your boyfriend was standing there looking as handsome as could be. His skin, brown as a bean and you loved it. Your mom loved it as well because as he took a seat, your mom was blushing. Your little brother, who was sitting on the stairs ran down and said, "Oh shit dude, what's happening'? Give me some skin!" as he held out his hand flat. Your brother has always been obsessed with black people ever since he watched Soul Train, 106th and Park or the BET (Black Entertainment Television) channel. This day you will always remember because it was like one of those celebrity dance shows. Everyone was judging your boyfriend. You had two out of three approved votes but you needed one more from your dad. He did the unthinkable. When your boyfriend stuck his hand out to shake your dads hand, your dad had a horrible look on his face. It was a face that you have never seen him do before.

After your boyfriend ate dinner with your family, thanked them all for a great meal then departed, your dad said, "What the hell is that?" You didn't understand what he mean so you ask him to explain. "Why in the hell did you bring a black boy to my house?" Right then and there you knew that your father was racist. You decided to stand up to your father and stop his ignorant thoughts right in its tracks. "Dad, I don't like what you're saying. You don't sound like the smart person that I've always thought you were. You don't know anything about him and for you to factor in his skin color out of all things when first meeting him is stupid! You raised us up christian or catholic... you never make up your mind-- and for some reason you act like you're better than everyone else on the planet. As if you have a right to judge him by the color of his skin. Dad, you know absolutely nothing. Do you know your history? If it wasn't for that 'black boy' and his 'black people,' white people like us wouldn't exist. But you wouldn't know anything about that....now would you!? Since you don't, I'm going to waste my precious

time and teach you. And don't interrupt
me because you and every other racist
dad needs to know this. I said don't
interrupt me! For centuries, people like
you have implied that anything that's
black is wrong, bad, inferior or evil.
When in fact, it's the other way around.
For instance, the Mormon bible-- which
your best friend Phil believes in-- teaches
that people of a dark skin complexion, are
cursed by God and that's why their skin is
dark. It's called the Curse of Cain. How
can that be? That's implying that God is
ashamed of his own complexion and that
he too feels his skin is cursed. The
reason I say that is because we all know
that God created Man in his own image.
I took your advice and studied hard like

you always taught us to do. Stop! Don't say anything...just freaking listen for once! I was watching the National Geographic channel to learn a thing or two, when a documentary called Journey of Man came on. Spencer Wells, who is one of the best geneticist analyzed DNA from people in all regions of the world. He figured out that all humans alive today came from a single black man who lived in Africa like 60,000 years ago. He proved that Modern humans didn't start their spread across the globe until after 60,000 years ago. Therefore, if there were an Adam & Eve- they were black people from Africa!

In all of these different cultures and

religions, people say that Jesus is some white guy with blue eyes or something. It's kind of crazy because I have never come across any white person who has been accepted the fact that Jesus has nowhere near the same complexion as us.

Otherwise, the people who have come to grips with the fact that Jesus isn't the same color as us settle with the belief that Jesus is Middle Eastern. Can you tell that your racism bothers me?! Oh...and by the way it really bothers mom too! She doesn't say anything because you'll probably get all pissed off like you always do. Oh, and I guess I should bring this to your attention now: your son....yeah well he thinks he black. At school, he tells everyone to call him 'white chocolate' instead of Tyler-- as you named him. Back to the subject...

Anyway... people saying that Jesus is from the Middle East must give them some kind of sense of satisfaction because nowadays, a lot of the people out there have a "tanned" look. As long as white people can get "tanned" enough to reach the same color as the so-called race Jesus and his people were, then they're happy!

The bible is filled with soooo many lies, Dad!. Go tell Phil that Jesus was born in Africa. I can pretty much guarantee that the first thing he'll say is, "No, he's from the Middle East. He was born in Jerusalem." That response means; "No, Jesus isn't black and he's not from Africa, where black people come from."

Everyone wants to believe that Jerusalem is on the other side of the world! Jerusalem is right on the borderline of Africa. And the borderline didn't even exist until a few white guys began colonizing about 400 years ago and deciding what area is what and who it should belong to. So instead of keeping Africa the size that it originally was, they made a line on the ground where Jesus was born and said, '...that side is Africa where the black people are from and this side will be considered the Middle East, where fair skinned people now reside. Of course, after the migration of jet black, dark skinned Africans that you despise-- evolved into Middle Eastern looking people.

Do you see how the truth is being twisted? Jesus hid with the dark black Africans in Egypt to keep safe from King Herod, who wanted him dead. That means he had to fit the description of the people he was hiding with because a pale, blue eyed, wavy haired person wouldn't be very camouflaged when in the middle of a bunch of dark-skinned, black eyes, thick wooly hair, Africans. Don't you agree? I really hope so...

Dad, why didn't you teach me this

anyways??? Why did I have to figure all of this out on my own? Why did I have to watch the Oprah show to find out the fucking truth!? All you ever do is lie. You lie about everything! Dad, I cannot comprehend your reaction to my boyfriend....you are really giving me a stomach ache. Didn't you say one of your closest high school friends was black? Or was that a lie too? You know what....you're not even listening. And that's okay....you're the one who is going to live your whole life close minded and not knowing. I'm going to my room and I'm locking my door." After all those long talks about never judging a book by its cover, it was finally clear. Your father was a liar who pretended to be the great

man that you thought he was. Your
boyfriend called later that night and your
dad answered the phone. "Please don't
call here anymore boy," he said to your
boyfriend. As you hear your father
destroy the best thing in your life, you
hurt inside. How? Why? Since when?
All of these thoughts and answers begin
to run through your mind about your dad.
Your mom remains silent even though
she knows its dead wrong because he
might start a fight with her. The way he
transformed into a different person after
meeting your boyfriend, makes you
second guess his character and what his
values really are. Even though you stood
up to your father and defended your
boyfriend-- things didn't turn out the way

you would've like them to. Wounds were
too deep. The next day at school you see
your boyfriend. You try to talk to him
but he walks away. He knows you have a
racist father but he doesn't want to hurt
your feelings and tell you that. Years
have passed and still you think of him
every single time you see a handsome
black guy. Your father is the reason why
you can't hold a relationship together.
No matter what, you will never have that
approval from your father that you want.
As you sit at home and read this... think
to yourself and say, 'I'm my own woman
and I love black men. I'm going to find
my perfect piece of dark chocolate and
marry him whether my old dad approves
or not!'

{Long Distance}

You may have met him on a family vacation. Or you may have known him since elementary school. The bottom line is that you both promised to always remember each other and reunite. You promised each other that the relationship that you were both invested in would never end. Even though the distance between the two of you was from coast to coast, you both truly believed that it would work. You talked on the phone 24/7. Every chance that you got, you would call him. You rang him during your lunch break at work. You talked to him while you took a bath. Before bed, you would call to say goodnight. Every night when you called to say 'sweet dreams,' you both would never want to say goodbye. Thinking like that, left you both sitting up on the phone all night, until you both fell asleep. Resting the phone on your cheek while laying on your side became a magical skill for you. To balance the phone on your face while slowly fading in and out of a deep sleep takes talent. Your relationship with him revolved around your cell phone. The land line in your home is what helped a lot. On those days where you forgot to charge your cell phone, that land line came in handy. When your cell phone battery pack became so hat that you couldn't even hold it anymore, you'd grab that land line that never over heated. It never cut out on your important times you spent talking to him. You both were pretty much glued to the phones! Having phone sex became a normal thing for the two of you. While creating a mental vision of him was enough for you, I can't say the same for him. That one night when you both got together for your monthly reunion, he tried to tell you. He tried to tell you that it is so difficult to make the relationship work. Every time he began to express to you how he was feeling, you would interrupt him. Excited to be with him in person, you'd probably say, "I missed you sooo much baby! I love you," repeatedly. With interruption and your kind words to follow....telling you how he was truly feeling wasn't going to happen. You have to remember, just because he didn't think the relationship would work out with the whole long distance thing-- doesn't mean he didn't love you. He cared about your feelings and that's why he did not continue to tell you how he was feeling. Anyhow, didn't you notice the guilty look on his face? Didn't you notice the slight change in his personality? I'm just saying, didn't you feel the vibe? If you are saying "no" to yourself right now, you need to replay the whole thing over in your head again! Actually, never mind. I'm sure you've done that over and over, time and time again.

I must admit, the way you had to find out about his change of heart was wrong. It was hurtful, disrespectful and very cowardly... in your eyes. Remember to see both sides of the story. After the kisses and hugs, he said goodbye and told you that he would call you as soon as the plane landed. You waited by the phone but you received no call. After calling his cell phone a half dozen times, he finally picked up. "Why didn't you call me when the plane landed? I was worried sick

about you," you said in a very upset tone.
He took a deep breath and silence
became the conversation. I know you
remember that silence from a distant lie
that you have told or a situation that you
have been in. Remember, you were the
silent one. "What's wrong and why are
you so silent?" Before you could even
finish asking that question, the answer
was already in your heart. Silence was
the conversation again. You knew it was
over, after he took another slow deep
breath and said, "I don't know what to
say?" "Don't say anything," you replied in
a heartbroken tone. As you took the land
line from your ear and slowly hung the
phone up, you heard a voice in the
background that sounded slightly

feminine. Instead of letting it roll off of your shoulder, you quickly picked the phone back up in hopes that he didn't hang up the phone yet. "She hung up," you heard him say as if he was talking to someone. Then he hung up the phone. Well, he didn't actually hang up all the way. He thought he did but he didn't. Knowing that you might hear some things that you probably wouldn't want to hear, you sat very quietly, holding your breath and listening in. "Why didn't you just tell her it was over and that you love me now?" "Oh stop it, Katie! I still love her. She's my closest friend and I would appreciate it if you weren't so rude," he said with anger in his voice. Knowing that another woman was in his life and that things were over between you both, hurt like hell but hearing how much he still cares made you feel better. After hearing that , you hung up the phone and cried. You cried your heart out, then you began to smile. You smiled because you knew for sure that the love your man had for you was real and still there...in a different way. You're right! He loves you and always will. The love that men give to their friends, always seems to be more intense than the love they shown towards a girlfriend. With that being said... be happy that he loves you as a friend. It means a lot more than what you may think.

Since then, he has tried to contact you

but you never return his calls. You changed your number because you knew how easy it would be to fall back in love with him. That was a very smart decision although the distance you created between the both of you turned permanent. But you know how the saying goes, "It's better to loved and lost than to have never loved at all." The bottom lines is that men need constant attention. Let the truth be told, men are just like women when it comes to being noticed. The only difference between a man and a woman's interpretation of being acknowledged is... a woman is happy with phone calls and being reminded how loved, beautiful and special they are. Men on the other hand need physical touch! Men need all five senses to be present at every moment. Hear, see, smell, touch and taste. Remember that.

{In With The New}

I'm so happy for you. You finally go rid
of the zero and got with a hero. Let's be
honest, you couldn't really see yourself
spending the rest of your life with him.
The only things that tied you both
together was one of three things:
children, sex or being afraid to be alone.
You both grew apart and that is
completely normal. Besides.... both of you

hated pretty much everything about each other. He hated your sarcasm and you hated his annoying grin. His smile was cute but his mean ways made him look so ugly. He stopped treating you like a queen and began to treat you like... nothing, pretty much. To him, your opinion didn't matter anymore! The only time he paid any attention to you was when it was time to have sex. As soon as his little wee wee started to think on its own, that's when you became "Mrs. Correct about everything." As long as his little ding-a-ling was pumping blood through it, you could get away with anything including murder. If he didn't agree or do what you said to.... he wasn't getting any of your va-jay-jay. I know it hurts to know that you were only being heard or cared about, only when it came to sex. You're worth more than that and you deserve better. The pointless arguments, name calling and nitpicking became very disturbing. Everything that involved you and him, just didn't work. Of course you will always have a special place in your heart for him but that's pretty much it. I know, I know, you both became too close and now you see him more so as a brother than a love, boyfriend, husband etc. Time is known to heal and also hurt. In your situation, time hurt your relationship. As time passed, you realized more and more about what kind of person he truly was. And he was completely different from you.

Compatibility.... uh no! His unpredictable mood swings were way too much for you to comprehend. When you both finally decided to call it quits, that was the happiest day of your life. Little did you know, life isn't all peachy and perfect when it comes to relationships. See, splitting up with your ex was a good thing but that didn't mean that your next relationship would be perfect. After your break up, you instantly hit the dating scene. You were anxious to have sex with another man. You were anxious to see what they thought of you. With all of that fire between your legs, you set out to find that perfect guy. Finding that perfect guy wasn't as easy as you thought it would be. You found yourself feeling ashamed, dirty and even unworthy sometimes. After a little guidance from a few close friends, you realized that you were going about life in the wrong way. You came to the conclusion that you didn't need a man in your life in order to be happy. You can please yourself a lot better than any man can. Getting in touch with yourself and learning to value your morals, life began to flow like water. If you put out good energy into the universe, it will hit you right back with the exact same force. When you least expected it, you walked right into the man of your dreams. At first, you didn't really like him that much but that powerful force ended up bringing you both together for one reason or another.

After the fourth time of randomly running into him and being asked out, you said "yes" to meet up for coffee. From there, the rest was history. You both are still together and the relationship is going strong. It's been over three years and everyday still feels the same as it did when you both first met. The moral, go do the right thing and follow your heart. Get out with the old and get in with the new!

{He's out of His Mind}

So, what ever happened to that guy that you met at the grocery store? You know... that guy who happened to be walking down the exact same aisle as you were consecutively. That guy who acted like he was interested in Kashi cereal, just because he saw you reading the nutrition facts on the back of the box. You know who I'm talking about. He wasn't the most handsome of men but his smooth lines and funny comments made him just as good looking. When you met him, you noticed he was wearing a wedding ring but you paid it no mind because a friendly conversation never hurt anyone. He asked you what your interest were. You responded with saying, "I don't really do much. I work all day and by the time I get off... I'm dead tired. I have to force myself to get up and go to the gym." That response gave him all of the answers that he needed to know. Working all day indicates that you're a hard worker. It also indicated that you're focusing on you and your career. No room for a husband, boyfriend or even kids. With that in mind, he started to blast you with reasons why you needed a break. "If you don't take a break, you'll drive yourself crazy." Or how about this one, "Oh, you're one of those workaholic types, huh?" The first comment is very true, so you begin to consider relaxing and taking a few days off for yourself for that following week. The second comment is something you didn't want to be known as because most of those kinds of people are self-centered. To make sure that this total stranger didn't feel that way about you, you replied with this... "You're right, I'm going to take a few days off next week to just relax." Wrong move sweet heart! That reply left you wide open, literally. "That's good... I actually know of a great burger joint downtown. Would you like to go get something to eat on your day off?" Stuck between a rock and a hard place, you say, "Sure." Numbers are exchanged and that following week, you receive his phone call.

At noon on a weekday, you both meet at that burger joint he mentioned to you at the grocery store. He was right... that burger tasted fantastic! That made you trust him a little more. You both sat down on the bench near the small burger place and enjoyed eating and talking. This time around, you noticed that he didn't have on his wedding ring. One day he's wearing it and the next... he's not. A little suspect, don't you think? Again, you paid it no mind because it wasn't any of your business. Worrying about his personal life would make eating burgers a little more personal than you would have liked. He obviously caught you looking down at his hand in deep thought, so to cover his ass he says, "Wow, I forgot my wedding ring inside of my gym locker." He was so nonchalant about the whole situation, you overlooked that as well. Not giving it a second thought, somehow the conversation changed to a different topic. The question is, why is a married man taking a single woman out to lunch? The other question is... is he really married?

After talking about your favorite late

night shows, you finally decided to ask him that big question that has been bothering you ever since the first day you guys met at the grocery store. "Are you married? Do you have a wife?" His response may have been one of the three. 1.) "Yeah, actually I am. Why? Does that bother you or something? 2.) "I was married but we are separated now because I caught her cheating on me with another man." 3.) No, we aren't married anymore. We haven't been intimate in years. We sleep in different rooms and I still wear my wedding ring because it's hard for me to take it off. It's hard for me to move on." Hearing that last statement could only do one thing and that's make him sound like a loving, helpless, caring guy who wants to be loved. We all know those are the three things that women always fall for. Women are naturally caring creatures, so if someone or something is vulnerable, a woman will do any and everything to help. In this case, you wanted to help him feel better about himself and his situation... so you placed your hand on top of his. Not smart of you. While you thought you were trying to console him and help him feel better about the sensitive subject that you decided to bring up, he took it in a completely different sort of way. In his mind, placing your hand on his, meant that you wanted to live life with him and take on whatever struggles and future plans he had in mind. You left that day thinking that you would never see that guy again. After finishing your burger and the long deep conversation, you said goodbye and told him thanks. By the time you made it home, there were over four voice messages on your answering machine. "Hey, just wanted to say I had a great time." "Can we get together tomorrow?" "Sorry to call again but I just wanted to talk, you know?" "Okay, this is the last time I'll call." After listening to those messages... you begin to worry a little bit. A few days go by and not a received call or text message. Assuming that this guys crush is over, you go to work feeling good and rejuvenated.

Before entering the building doors that

you work in, a guy approaches you out of the blue. Before you could have the chance to identify him, he was already greeting you. "Hey! I tried calling but I got your answering machine every time!", he says while leaning in for a hug. Shocked by his greeting, you kind of pull back. Looking up at him and getting a good look, you say, "What are you doing here?" No response from him, just a weird smile on his face. "I gotta get inside for work. I'm running late." As you walk into the building, you turn to take a quick look back to make sure he's not following you. Instead of following you, he does something much more creepy. He stood still and watched you until you were out of sight with a big smile on his face. You told everyone at your work place about him and they said that you should get a restraining order or something. You didn't go with that idea because he didn't actually do anything bad. Very weird but not bad.

Anyway, he continued to call for weeks on end, leaving voice messages. After about a month of calling and receiving the voice mail greeting, he started just hanging up the phone on the message machine. Shit got even more crazy! He left flowers on your doorstep, while you were out of town visiting you new boyfriend. You told your boyfriend about him and asked him to come stay with you in your apartment for a couple weeks so that your stalker would see that you have a man. That idea worked perfectly. While you and your new boyfriend were out on the town, you saw him at the bar drinking by himself. From across the room, he noticed you and your man snuggled up, kissing and hugging. Your stalker could have reacted one of two different ways after seeing you kissing a guy. He could have easily got pissed off and turned more psycho or he could have seen you both together and backed off. He decided to back off because he knew that your new boyfriend would kick his ass if he didn't.

The next time you are in a store and a random guy walks up to you, please don't give him any time of day. Meeting in a grocery store isn't the ideal meeting place for hopeful dating opportunities.

{Can't Buy Love}

Hey! Hey! Hey!!! Stop buying that guy all of those damn gifts. Stop giving him all of your hard earned money. Last but not least, stop letting him drive your car and stay gone for days at a time. You don't have to give or buy gifts in order to be loved. That sexy guy is not worth you going broke. That sexy v-shaped guy, is not worth your happiness. Stop calling him and asking if he would like to come over. Let him ask you if he could come over. Once a man figures out that you're needy, he will take advantage of that. Using your weakness against you, will become the goal. Look... if a guy actually goes off and drives your car somewhere, stays gone for a long period of time, returns back with nothing... that's a problem. When I say "nothing," I mean... if he doesn't come back with a job, new way of thinking or hope in his heart. Have you noticed that he only calls you when he needs something? Lets put it this way.... the majority of men have selfish intentions. Not all men, but most. Stop letting him use you. You may enjoy sex with him but trust me, sex isn't everything! Sex is just a small piece of a relationship when you really think about it. At the moment you may feel in need of a male presence but again.... it's not worth it. The times that you both spent sitting on the couch together watching a movie, may have been great but he was most likely anxiously waiting for the movie to end so intercourse could take place. After intercourse, both of you fall asleep. When you awake... he will be gone and so will your vehicle. Damn, this whole situation is funny to me because women will say, "Screw off!" to all of her friends and family for a complete asshole of a guy. And the bottom line, is because of neediness and fear of being alone. Get over that hump, girlfriend. A man doesn't

complete you or make you any better of a
woman. All of that starts within you!!!
Hello!! Can I get an Ah-Men!!
Hall-- e-- lujah!!

{Good Guy Gone Bad}

Believe it or not, he was once a good guy. He held doors for ladies. He cooked dinner for his lover. He also told her how much he cared. Everyday was heaven for him and he made sure it was the same for her. At night, he would tell her all of his deepest darkest secrets, fears and thoughts. The word love can't explain the feelings that he had for her. Often his

lover would dance to the music that he
played on his guitar. Everything they did
was done together. He often cried in
front of her because he felt that it was
okay. When they went out to dinner, he
paid the tab every single time because it
made him feel good inside. At night
before bed, he ran her bath water for her
and even lit candles all around the tub.
He washed her back and got her bed
clothes ready for her with nightwear
nicely folded on the bed waiting perfectly
for his lover. He would leave the room to
give her some space and alone time.
Basically, he lived for her. Both of her
parents loved him and his charming
ways. All of this took a turn for the worst
after she went back to visit her

hometown for a few weeks. This is a story that he never told you because he would rather not think about it. His heart was broken into two pieces. Anyhow, while she was away... a fire rekindled between her and an older guy that she had a big crush on back in her high school days. The story is that she went over to his mothers house to say "hello" since their families were close friends. The bad part is that he still lived with his mom and never left the nest. They meet eyes and the rest is history. She threw away real love for a one night stand. When he received news, he called many of his friends balling his eyes out. Amongst his friends was me. I heard the hurt in his voice. I felt his pain and the anger he had in his heart for women was undeniable. "I can't believe she would fuck some guy! What the fuck was she thinking? She told me that she loved me. She looked me directly in my eyes and said that she would never lie to me. That was bullshit man!!! She's a fucking liar. That stupid lying whore! I gave her everything! I gave her my heart. What ever she wanted, I gave and I loved every second of it. I can't believe I trusted her. I was so stupid to have thought she really cared. Dude, my heart hurts so bad. You don't understand... I literally want to fucking kill her! A part of me feels dead... from here on out, it's bros before hoes. I will never, I mean never, never ever fall for another chick again." From that day forth, it was a load of head games for every woman that he has come in contact with. He stopped sparing their feelings and started sparing his own. Telling women whatever they wanted to hear in order to get what he wanted became the model. Love ended that night heart was broken by his ex-girlfriend.

So, please don't take it personal. That's just how he decided to deal with the pain. You could be the perfect woman but he won't see it because his heart is still broken. It's been so long, being a player to him is now a lifestyle. It's a mask that he can't take off. And if he ever does reveal his true self, it will take a hell of a woman and a shit load of time to open

him up. We all want to be free. Free
from pain that hurts us all mentally,
physically and emotionally. Bottom line,
he's broken. Fix him if you'd like!

{Black Girl Booty}

"Who is that? Do you know her?
Why is she here? Where is she from and
how long is she going to be here? She
has a nice butt. Do you like her butt?"
These are all of the questions that you
had running though your mind for your
man as *she* walked by. You wanted to
ask him if he liked black girls so bad but
you decided to hold back and watch him

as he watched her. As she walked by
with her naturally tanned golden brown
skin, wearing stilettos and a business
suit.. it made you wonder. She wasn't the
typical black girl that you see on rap
videos. She walked with such
confidence. It seemed as if the ground
beneath her felt privileged to be stepped
on. Her skirt hugged her hips, thighs and
booty perfectly. The sight that you saw
on her was the look that you were hoping
your man saw on you that day when you
tried on your new outfit. You remember,
don't you. You turned around in a
complete circle, sliding your hands down
the side of your hip, feeling the texture of
your dress and making sure it was fitting
right. After asking him, "How does this

outfit look on me honey?" about five times, he finally responded with this, "It looks good... very good. Now can you move over a little bit so I can see the TV? The game is on and you keep interrupting." You could have been wearing nothing and he wouldn't have paid you any mind. Well.... maybe I'm exaggerating a little. If you were naked then he would have noticed, lol. Guys have x-ray vision when it comes to naked. That's funny. A guy can see a fully clothed woman and see right through the clothes. That's just a mans imagination. That's exactly what your man was doing when he saw that black chick walk by. I know it upset you to see him actually checking out a black girl. What you forgot is that guys see no color when sex appeal is in front of him. That black girl could have been lime green and if she had the exact same shape, the exact same jaw dropping reaction would have occurred. This is the God's honest truth. Just think about it, white men being attracted to black, Indian, Vietnamese women... has been going on for hundreds and hundreds of years. Remember that part of history your teachers left out about how the white men would leave his white wife to make babies with the African slave woman? What about your great grandpa who married a Vietnamese woman while being stationed in Vietnam? See, what I think happened to you is... you fell for the stereotypes that

America created and wants so badly to be true. White women with white men, makes a perfect couple and family. That's not what makes a perfect couple or family. The diversity is what makes us beautiful. In my opinion, too much of one color becomes a big blaaah to me. I like to see all races and nationalities dating, marrying and having children. There is no better way to improve yourself than to become one with someone who is the complete opposite of yourself. So stop thinking, "He won't like a black girl," or "He doesn't like Chinese girls." Better yet, stop feeling entitled and thinking that you're the only thing he wants because you're both white. Like I said before.... sex appeal has no color. To answer all of your thoughts that you were having when you saw that black girl with the nice booty walk by. "Who is that?" Hell if he knows, he's just as surprise as you are. "Did he know her?" Hell no, but I think he wouldn't mind. "Where is she from?" Beats him. "Does he think she has a nice butt?" You know what, I'm going to let you answer that question for yourself. If you thought she had a nice ass, don't you think he did too??? But just because he thinks a woman is sexy, doesn't mean he wants to marry her or wants to leave you for her. Men are just very visual creatures.

{Kiss and Tell}

I think everyone hates a kiss and tell. Especially when you don't want to be known as a hoe. For some reason a kiss always leads to a touch and a touch leads to something else more inappropriate. Honestly, you deserved to be called those horrible names like, "Hoe with the tramp stamp." The reason I say it's your fault for the name calling is

because you could have easily avoided
the whole situation. Before you took
those sexual acts as far as what you did,
something in the back of your mind said,
"What the hell are you doing?" In
response to your little voice, was a reply
of stupidity, lust and lack of respect for
yourself. That stupid voice, which most
likely was the devil talking said, "You
better pull your pants down and get
freaky!" Cool, cool, you did some nasty,
sexual things with a guy who just left
another girls house after doing the exact
same thing with her. She probably was
your best friend, lol. After the devils
persuasion got the best of you, you found
yourself sitting there thinking about the
probability you may have of now

contracting an STD or infection. Women are supposed to have the will power and when you give in... you always lose. You may feel like you didn't do anything wrong but in reality, you did. Your actions will forever be with you. Your dirty and unprepared actions will cause you problems for the rest of your life. Honestly... guys want to marry a clean woman. Clean, meaning untouched, pure and respectful. So if you're sitting around wondering why you're not married... just count in your head, all of the men that you have done sexual things with. Times that number by 1000. Don't you get it? Guys simply kiss and tell. There is no way around it. Like I said before... you could have avoided it all. Now you're probably thinking, "Shit, I guess I'm not telling the next guy that I date, about my past relationships." Right? Well, let me give you a little advice about that conclusion. That's a bad idea because for some reason, guys always know other guys. The word will get around. Seriously, you could have sexed up a guy in Maine and sexed up another guy in Timbuktu and sooner or later, they will meet somehow. Why does that always happen? I don't know? Could it be because guys always kiss and tell? I think so. So next time you find yourself horny, be smart because the outcome is not worth it. Besides, it's a horrible feeling when you find out that he really didn't give a shit about you anyway. Sexual acts are for people who are in love. That's funny because that rule only applies to women. It makes me think, how can sexual things ever happen if guys always play games and pretend to care? I think if you took the time to contemplate for a while, you would know if a guy really cared or not. Let's be honest though... most of the time this saying is on point. "It ain't cha beauty... it's ya booty."

{He likes Old Ladies!}

Okay, yes he likes older women! He
thinks older women are sexier than all
hell! But lets get this straight, he doesn't
like old, old women, like you always try to
make it sound. It's not like he checks out
Grandmas or anything. I think you
always over exaggerate the age of the
older women that you catch him
checking out because that's all you can

say about the women. Since you're younger than her, you use the whole age thing to throw in his face. "What the hell! Why are you checking out an old lady? That's nasty!" You attempt to make him feel stupid or bad for finding an older woman to be sexy. Hearing you say all of those mean things about her, the lady that you don't know... reassures him that she was indeed, truly hot! If she wasn't good looking like you say, then you would not have been so bothered by the whole thing. Young men love older women. The same way older women love younger men. Why do young men love older women? Umm... I think it's because older women seem to care more about their appearance overall. They show it in a very subtle mature manner. Older women are very wise and young men need that. Older women never tear down and I think that's because they have lived long enough to understand that trying is all a person can do. Knocking someone down while trying to advance is something that most older women do not condone. See, that is why young men like older women. Also, because they cook every night. We all know the key to a mans heart is through his stomach. Since we are on the top of young men who like older women, let me give you some more reasons. It's something about the way they carry themselves. They seem to never be in a hurry. Raising their voice, getting snappy and upset with you is a rare thing. Honestly, you could learn a thing or two from older women if you would just observe. Demi Moore should have been the first person who came to your mind when I said that. Seriously!!!! Young men love older women that take good care of themselves. So, if you're an older woman and you're reading this... you most likely already know what I'm taking about. This is all true, so if you really want to know... here it is. Your man does think older women are hot and so does every other young man on the planet!! Therefore, stop with the snappy remarks. He's just being who he is. Which is a horn dog, trying to figure himself out.

{Break Up}

A break up is never easy. As a matter of fact, it's probably one of the most difficult things that a person will go through or be faced with besides death. There is no explanation that can describe the feeling a death of a loved one can cause. A break up is similar to a death because during a divorce/break up the mind, body and soul truly believes that a part of them is dying. Either way, it's loving and losing. The only difference between a break up and a death is, a death is forever and a break up is always determined by the individuals-- if they'd like to get back together. Here's where I'm going with this. If you break up with a person, make sure you are certain because if you're not and you decided to enter the relationship again... your man will take advantage of you. You coming back to the relationship is a sign of weakness. Although that is not true on all occasions, it is on most. Let him run back to you. Don't wait on him too long to make a decision because all males have short attention spans. He will forget about you if another beautiful woman

steps in. Actually, he won't completely
forget about you but while he's with that
new woman, he will. It's always good to
make your man wait but just not too long.
Waiting makes a man want you more.
Don't call him all the time but if you're on
the phone with him, make sure that the
conversation is all about him and nothing
else. Remember I told you about the
whole stroking a mans ego and how you
can always benefit from it? Okay, now
apply!!!

{Big Girls}

Many of you really fit, skinny and petite women always assume that you will get the guy over a big girl. You actually think that big girls have no chance, don't you? Be honest! Don't sit here and lie to me or yourself. Is that why you always bring your "big girl" friend along whenever you're going to meet up with some cute guys? It's

because you want all of the attention.
You want to be the star.... right? If being
praised by the opposite sex is wrong, then
I don't want to be right and neither
should you. With that being said, don't
let being beautiful close your mind to
what reality is. Reality is knowing that
just because someone weighs more than
you, doesn't mean that hot guy won't go
for the other girl. Don't get me wrong.
Please don't get me wrong! Men love sex
and a pretty body to look at-- but who
says men don't like a woman with a little
meat on her bones?? Huh, who says
that?? I think meat on a woman's bones
is very sexy! Oh and guess what? I'm a
hot guy!!!! Boys like girls who are very
seductive but listen very closely....men

like women who are very loving. Think about that one. How about this. Guys date ladies who put out but men date women who open up. Think long and hard about that. This is what I have been taught about women my whole life. I don't know if this is true but this is what my father told me. The very pretty, sexy and in shape women are truly the ones that men shouldn't go for because they don't keep up with good hygiene. "The pretty girls get the guys all the time and that makes them cocky. When a person gets cocky, they begin to feel like they don't have to take care of themselves anymore. Why would they have to take very good care of themselves if they can get whatever guy they want? Watch and see.... pretty girls don't take as many showers as big girls or not so pretty girls do. That's because pretty girls just throw on some make up and call it a day. "Big girls," they understand that they rarely get any attention from men so they do any and everything to look, smell and feel pretty enough to catch an eye. A big girl will please her man while a pretty girl will think that you have to cook for her every night! So, don't ever judge a book by it's cover. You'll understand when you get a little older." That's what my dad told me on a regular basis. Surprisingly, a lot of that has been true. Shit, I like big girls! There's nothing wrong with a big girl. Big girls need love too. And guess what, there is a lot of hot guys out there who give it to them. Be proud to be a Big, Big Girl! Shake what ya mama gave you‼ If people don't like the way you are... then they can just screw off!

{Love & Work}

Here I go with my examples. First, I have a question. Why in the world did you date a man that works with you? Dating men that work with you is the worst thing that you can do. Don't try to explain, I already know what you were about to say. "It wasn't supposed to go that far," right?

He transferred from a small law firm in
Arkansas to the same company you
worked at in New York City. When he
first arrived, he looked like a lost puppy.
You could tell that the New York fast life
would swallow him whole if he wasn't
careful. The law firm that you worked for
was a lot more up-tempo than the firm
that he arrived from. At the beginning,
you promised yourself that you wouldn't
get romantically involved with anyone at
work. You're very certain that it would
not happen but just when you thought
everything was clear... you were assigned
to work a case with him. You both met
up at the cafe to discuss all of the
different court stuff. Time spent is time
spent! Most of that time that you both

spent together discussing the case was a little bit more than just co-workers. You often looked in his eyes and saw his kind soul. One night, after a few too many drinks, while discussing the case at his empty apartment, you kissed him. Quickly after the incident, you blamed it on the liquor.

The relationship made great progress and you were infatuated with the fact that you were more than he has ever been with. You found yourself screwing him just because! You knew he loved it. In your mind, him being from Arkansas was assurance that he has never had a freak like you. Women out there stayed still during sex like a log floating in the middle of the lake. No emotion, passion or fire. That alone made you want him more and more. You just wanted to show off your bedroom skills.

While you moved and grooved with him every chance you got, he fell in love more and more. Love... that was the last thing on your mind. Satisfying your own personal problems by proving that you're a good lover was very close minded of you. That boy from Arkansas, thought the relationship was real! He didn't know that he was nothing more than a tool. After you realized that he was really falling for you, you decided to stop seeing him and that broke his heart in two.

From that day forth, work was an uncomfortable place to be because he would look at you like you took away his ability to care ever again. You broke his heart and you also lost a good friend. Only if you could have been a little bit stronger and resisted the temptation. Don't ever do that to yourself ever again because it's not worth it. It will be a very long time before he forgives you. If you would like to make up for your action... all you have to do is ask. He will understand.

{Granny Panties}

This is a serious topic. Very serious! So listen. It seems that many of you Grandmothers out there don't have your priorities straight. Maybe it could be because of... forget that, there's no reason for your actions. You're a grandmother. You have kids and grandchildren that you place behind random men and your "career." Correct me if I'm wrong but that is not something that a grandmother should do. Your main focus should be your grandchildren and not satisfying your need to have a male presence around you. You jump from man to man and bed to bed, trying to find love. Come on now... that kind of love should be completely out of your mind. Warm love should be the only love that you have inside. The love of life. The love of earth. The love of family! That's the love you should possess. Not sexual love! You have lived your glory day and now time is ticking. You owe the rest of your little bit of years of living to your children and grandchildren. You were married once and that failed. Why? How? When? All of those questions don't matter anymore. Again, you have children and young grandchildren to tend to. Grandmothers, how do you go for so long not seeing or talking to your grandchildren? My grandmother was the complete opposite of the grandmothers now a days. She put us first. We never saw her with a man. That's even after her husband left her with five children to raise. She has been celibate (from what I know) since my mom was 5 years old. My mom is now 50 years old. No man! She was focused on what really mattered! She didn't need a man. The only love she wanted was from her family. I love her for that!!! Women need to go back to the basics. Being a hoe is not cool. Maybe you don't consider being with over six different guys in a matter of seven years as hoe like, but I do. Especially when you're a grandmother. Doing what you're doing is only going to lead to real unhappiness. The family and children that once loved you will no longer care. In time, you will be nothing more than a distant memory. That's really sad because... time cannot be rewound. It just keeps going forward, with or without you. So, use your time on this earth wisely. After you leave, you can't come back. Death is forever. Just something to think about.

Take pride in your granny panties.

{Long Lasting Love}

You both were together since the age of 13 years old. The same person who you made children with was the same person who you received your first kiss from. After school, you both would stay on school grounds and cuddle near the lockers. Then he would walk you half way home. Just half way because your dad would kill you if he knew that you were seeing a boy. Every time he would walk you home, he would carry your school books. If for some reason you wanted to carry your own things, he would insist on it. Remember going to the show and watching that highly anticipated movie that you both wanted to see? Better yet, do you remember sitting at the drive-in? That was a time to remember, wasn't it? Remember watching the stars together? Do you remember the long conversations about nothing? In high school, you both sat in the library together during lunch so you could configure your class schedules to match for the following semester. You promised each other that you both would stay together forever. Both of you cried together, smiled together and even ignored each other sometimes. Often you both would disagree with one another. Arguments would escalate into yelling and then you would storm into the room with a load of hatred in your heart. "I hate you! You're so stupid! Don't talk to me! Why do you always think you're right?!" But deep down inside, you both knew that the harsh words that were exchanged meant nothing more than just angry emotion. At times, you hated each other so much. It takes love to hate. Remember starting your own company together. At first you thought it would be a bad idea since you both did disagree on a lot of things. Surprisingly, the company did very well. Thanks to his ideas and

your computer savvy skills. Raising your
kids the best way you knew how was
your way of showing them love. Your
husband felt the same way. And that you
did. You raised your children to be very
respectful and considerate to others.
Although sometimes you may not feel
appreciated... you should know that they
love you. Your husband began to get sick
a lot for the past few years. Not too long
ago, he died. No "goodbye." No "I'll see
you in the morning." No "I love you." No
nothing. I can't begin to imagine how
much that must hurt your heart. I know
you cry when you are all alone. Your
heart drops into your stomach every time
you think of him. The late night
conversations replay in your head over

and over again. His smile... makes you happy. He often shows up in your dreams to say hello and to make sure you're still keeping strong. Every time he does show up, life feels great! I don't know if you truly understand just how much he loved you. He loved you when the arguing got bad. He loved you when you thought he hated you. He loved you then and he loves you now. Remember that.

{Pothead Boyfriend}

When you first met him, you liked him because everyone thought he was cool. Everywhere you went with him, people would always walk up to him and say hi. Even gangster looking black guys would scream his name from across the street and say, "Yo! Yo! What's up my nigga! Get at me playa!" Your boyfriend would smile and respond with "For sure, bro!!" Things like this made you wonder how and why he was so popular? You knew that he was a very nice guy overall but when has being a "nice guy" ever made someone popular? When you guys attended parties together, he would often hotbox with a few people. Sitting in a car with the windows rolled all the way up and smoking weed happened on a regular basis. You would not participate because you thought that smoking weed was stupid. So one night when you went over to your boyfriends house, he was smoking a joint. He looked over at you and held the joint out. "Take a hit," he said. You shook your head and said, "No thanks. You know I don't smoke." He replied with, "Whatever, more for me."

He continued to puff and puff as he watched cartoons. Looking over at him, you realized that being together with a person like that was not a good thing. You hated to watch him sit still like a zombie. When the weed kicked in, his eyes would turn really red and he kind of looked like a devil. Him ravaging through the cabinets for food like a wild animal didn't make it any less believable. Bottom line, his actions changed whenever he got high. You hated it so you broke up with him.

Weeks later, you saw him with another girl. The only difference is that she seemed to be really happy with him all of the time. You didn't understand this.

Why is she so damn happy? Why are they acting like they're in love when they have only been together for a week? Seeing them slobber all over each other actually made you jealous didn't it? Being jealous, is something that you shouldn't be. Him and her belong together because they both don't see a future for themselves and they don't understand that sitting around all day smoking weed will do nothing but kill brain cells. "The already half dead brain cells." While you go off to college or more forward in life, they will both be sitting in the same spot, doing the same thing. The blessing is that you had the strength to realize what was wrong and took the correct action. Don't let him get you down. Get yourself up and keep moving. There are many fish in the sea. He was just the fish who jumped out of the water on purpose.

Questions
& Answers

Q: Hi David, my boyfriend and I were together for two years. Then out of the blue, he decides that we shouldn't be together anymore. What should I do? I want to piss him off really bad! Thanks, Katie

A: If I were you, I would play it cool and just let it go. Cooler heads always prevail. Besides, if you don't react, that will make him wonder why? Then all kinds of things will run through his head. Okay, if you want to really upset him... here's what you should do. You find out a place that you know he will be and show up with a really cut black guy. Not just any black guy! This black guy must be very sharp, well spoken and physically fit. If he's sharp, when your ex introduces himself with a smart allic joke to follow, he will know how to respond promptly. He has to be well spoken because most people think that all black guys speak with ebonics. When a person speaks with ebonics, people do not think that person is educated. When someone is uneducated, others automatically feel superior for some reason. Now, being physically fit is a big deal because men are nothing more than muscles. You want to dominate your ex in every way that matters to him. If all fails, you can say... "My new black boyfriend can kick your ass!" That statement alone will strip him of his manhood because we are physical creatures. Being the toughest matters to us. Without it... we are nothing. :) Let's face it, all races of men are afraid of black guys, lol. With that being said, you can't go wrong with a very sharp, well spoken and physically fit black guy.

-David

Q: David, my name is Scott and I wanted
to know how I should approach a girl that
I like. I've been liking her since my
freshman year. I'm a senior now. Do you
have any ideas?

A: Wow, that's a hard one. First and
foremost, be completely honest. Be
yourself and remain cool, calm and
collected. Here's what I would do. I
would approach her when she is alone.
Catch her walking to class and run up
behind. Don't startle her. Make sure you
say her name before you get within five
feet of her so that you don't creep her out.
Say, "My name is Scott and I wanted to
say that I think you are really hot. I know
this is kind of random but I wanted to let

you know." Don't slow down in stride. Keep you pace and pass her up if you need to. That makes it seem as if you're busy. It also indicates that you truly told her that because you happened to notice her on your way to class. Don't wait for a response. Don't look back and keep going about your business. While in class, she will think of you and your nice words. From there, your in the door. Next time you see her, just walk right by without saying a word or any eye contact. That will make her wonder about you even more. Give it about a week and then spark up a friendly conversation. Ask about her weekend? That should work.

I hope that helps.

-David

Q: Hi there, I work from 9-5 and I haven't been on a date in years. Maybe it's because I'm too busy but I also don't think I'm letting off an inviting vibe. My question for you is, how should I go about finding a date?

Tara

A: Finding a date can be a hard thing to do sometimes. I would advise you to not go around looking or expecting for every man you chat with to ask you out. Letting off "stay away from me" vibes can be a big part of your not being asked out. You're probably not meaning to give off that vibe but I did read your email very carefully. Working from 9-5 every day will put an uninviting look on anyone's face. You're tired and in need of some rest. If I were you, I would make myself available by attending friendly get togethers with friends, co-workers and etc. You can be single but it doesn't mean anything unless someone else knows. Casual dating is very easy. It's nothing more than just being social.

-David

Q: My boyfriend wants to have sex with me and I don't know if I should. Should I?

A: First of all, if you're having doubts about having sex then you definitely shouldn't. If your boyfriend can't accept that, then he doesn't really care about you. I think you should wait until you truly care for someone before you decide to have sex. If you were my daughter, I would tell you not to have sex until you're married. That's the best advice I can give you. Boys are going to always be here. Take your time and choose wisely.

-David

Decoded

COMING SOON:

The Will To Survive

based on a true story

"David's voice is strong. He has many interesting stories to tell and a lot to say."

-Random House Senior Editor, Heather Jackson

David L. Johnson, Jr

About the Author

David L. Johnson Jr. is a top selling author who recently wrote his first national book entitled, *Lost & Found: A Memoir.* After the success of *Lost & Found,* David met and spoke with many readers during his book signings. They often times had questions about life, family & relationships etc. This persuaded him to write *Decoded,* a book which focuses on dating, relationships and love.

David is now hard at work on his third book, *The Will To Survive.* You may check for updates and more on his website: www.DavisBoyPublishing.com

When David is not writing, he enjoys spending time and having fun with his family as well as playing and coaching basketball.

To contact him with any questions or concerns regarding *Decoded,* please visit: www.DecodedBook.com

LaVergne, TN USA
13 September 2010
196845LV00001B/76/P